1. Introduction

U.S. corporations have been investing approximately $66 billion per year in direct foreign investments since 1990, and currently own and operate more than $1.1 trillion of assets abroad.[1] Corporate multinationality has been the subject of considerable research ever since U.S. direct foreign investment expanded rapidly in the 1960s, yet evidence on the effects of multinationality remains puzzlingly mixed.[2] This paper therefore examines an extensive data set of domestic and multinational corporations (DCs and MNCs) in order to more clearly establish the effects of multinationality on firm value. Our sample, measurement of multinationality, and use of control variables each is more comprehensive than previous work. Using up to 42,529 firm-year observations for U.S. nonfinancial corporations over the period 1984 through 1997, we find strong evidence that capital markets (over this time period) have consistently penalized multinationality by putting a lower relative value on the equity of MNCs than on otherwise similar DCs. We refer to this effect as the *multinational discount*. Our main contributions are to provide new evidence that: (1) convincingly documents the existence of the multinational discount; (2) suggests that multinationality causes, and is not merely associated with, the discount; (3) identifies foreign assets, at least in part, as the source of value destruction; and (4) links the pursuit of multinationality to an empire building motive of managers who don't own much of the firm.

Specifically, we find that, controlling for firm size, leverage, and industry, the market value of multinational firms is low in relation to assets and book value, and low -- but not quite as low -- in relation to earnings. Based on Tobin's q (the ratio of the market value of equity plus debt to the book value of assets), the multinational discount is in the range of 8.6% to 17.1%. Using the more

---

[1] The data are reported in the *Survey of Current Business*, July 1999.

[2] Errunza and Senbet (1981, 1984), Fatemi (1984), Doukas and Travlos (1988), and Morck and Yeung (1991) find that multinationality creates value for shareholders; Christophe (1997) finds that multinationality destroys value; Brewer (1981) finds no significant difference between multinational and domestic firms; Bartov, Bodnar, and Kaul (1996) and Reeb, Kwok, and Baek (1998) find that multinationals are riskier (which presumably lowers market value); while Hughes, Logue, and Sweeny (1975), Agmon and Lessard (1977), Brewer (1981), and Fatemi (1984) all report that multinationals are less risky (which presumably raises market value).

narrow ratio of book equity to market equity, the multinational discount is in the range of 3.5% to 9.7%, while the price/earnings ratio suggests a multinational discount in the range of 2.3% to 4.3%.

Our findings indicate that multinationality actually is associated with a slightly greater market value than an otherwise similar domestic firm, but is also associated with a dramatically higher asset size, by a ratio of 5 to 1, thus lowering q. Because the multinational discount is not as large relative to earnings, we can infer that the earnings of MNCs must be relatively low given their levels of assets. This suggests a link between assets, multinationality, and value destruction -- which we refer to as the *asset channel* of value destruction. It may be that multinationality destroys value because assets have to be relatively large for foreign projects in comparison to the earnings they generate, or that ROA is lower for the foreign projects that MNCs undertake. Alternatively, it may be that assets destroy value and multinationals happen to have large amounts of assets. We address this question of causation by showing that for a given level of assets, the greater the percent of those assets that are foreign, the lower the ROA.

The proposition that multinationality destroys value through an asset channel is consistent with a growing body of research revealing that other forms of diversification also destroy value. A *diversification discount* has been associated with industrial or product diversification, corporate conglomeration, and diversifying mergers. Denis, Denis, and Sarin (1997), Berger and Ofek (1995), Servaes (1996), and Lang and Stulz (1994) all show that corporate diversification results in value losses. Morck, Schleifer, and Vishny (1990) find that diversifying acquisitions decrease shareholder value. Our results appear to be related to these studies, which are suggestive that diversification is associated with extensive assets (or irreversible investments) that often do not generate a high (enough) return. On the flip side, asset sales, divestitures, and increases in corporate focus have been shown to benefit shareholders. Comment and Jarrell (1995) and John and Ofek (1995) both show that increased corporate focus results in shareholder value gains. With regard to multinationality, relatively little prior evidence exists. However, we provide new evidence that changes in multinationality are associated with changes in Tobin's q, such that increases in multinationality are associated with value destruction and decreases with value creation. This is consistent with the findings of Gleason, Mathur, and Singh (1999) who demonstrate that divestment of foreign assets by U.S. firms creates positive equity announcement effects.

2

Because the multinational discount appears closely related to the industrial diversification discount, we check that we are not simply capturing the same effect by proxy. In addition to controlling for the primary industry in which a firm operates, we therefore also add a control for product diversification. While product diversification is indeed associated with value destruction, we show that it does not affect the multinational discount. This evidence is consistent with the findings of Bodnar, Tang, and Weintrop (1997) and Morck and Yeung (1999).[3]

As additional support for our hypothesis that foreign assets destroy value in MNCs, we demonstrate that exporting, a substitute for multinationality which does not entail foreign assets, actually raises Tobin's q and thus creates value. Exporting is associated with a higher market value of the firm than an otherwise similar non-exporting firm, but also with a lower asset size of the firm (perhaps reflecting greater efficiency). This is consistent with the findings of Bernard and Jensen (1999) that exporters have superior performance across a variety of measures. Furthermore, our results indicate the multinational discount is unaffected by the exporting premium.

The evidence of a multinational discount leads us to consider why firms would become MNCs or increase their degree of multinationality. An "empire building" motive has been ascribed to managers who pursue value-destroying diversification because of private benefits (see, for instance, Denis, Denis, and Sarin (1997), Stulz (1990), or Jensen (1986)). Our evidence on the determinants of multinationality reveals that the greater the share of the firm owned by management, the less likely it is a multinational and the lower its degree of multinationality. We therefore conclude that managers of MNCs who do not own much of a firm may be constructing multinational empires to the detriment of shareholders. This finding is consistent with the similar relation found by Denis, Denis, and Sarin (1997) between management equity ownership and product diversification, as well as with the conclusion of Lang, Poulsen, and Stulz (1995) that management is reluctant to sell underperforming assets because they value firm size.

We also consider several alternative explanations for the multinational discount. First, we consider an exchange rate channel by estimating the impact of exchange rates on Tobin's q. Because

---

[3] Morck and Yeung (1999) report that measures of industrial and multinational diversification are positively correlated, but with low magnitudes, in the 0.17 region. Our measures are correlated with a magnitude of 0.09 to 0.29.

we have a relatively rich time-series dimension we are able to provide direct evidence that the market value (equity price) of MNCs varies inversely with the value of the dollar, where other studies, such as Christophe (1997), have only inferred this effect using sub-sample analysis. However, these foreign exchange effects do not explain the multinational discount, only that the discount is larger when the dollar is strong. Our analysis also reveals little impact from exchange rates onto ROA or earnings and we thus conclude that firms may be smoothing their income -- via accounting manipulations, financial hedging, or operational hedging -- but that the market (perhaps due to either more or less savvy) sees through this and adjusts the firm's equity prices accordingly.

A second alternative explanation for the multinational discount might be a possible risk channel of value destruction, whereby MNCs' exposures to foreign sources of (perhaps undiversifiable) volatility cause shareholders to discount their value. For example, Bartov, Bodnar, and Kaul (1996) illustrate that exchange rate variability increases the volatility of MNCs' equity prices. We find that MNC equity prices are indeed more volatile, and that the volatility appears attributable primarily to movements in the exchange rate. However, we do not find any evidence that volatility affects the level of Tobin's q. For instance, although fluctuations in the exchange rate affect the level of Tobin's q, we find that fluctuations in exchange rate *volatility* do not. Furthermore, we find that income-statement items, such as earnings, earnings per share, and sales are not more variable for MNCs, again suggesting that firms may be smoothing (or hedging) their income but that the firm's equity price nonetheless adjusts frequently. Hence, additional riskiness cannot explain the multinational discount.

As a third alternative explanation, we consider the impact of intangible assets, such as technological knowledge and brand names, on Tobin's q and the multinational discount. Consistent with previous studies (Morck and Yeung (1991) and Lang and Stulz (1994)), we capture intangible assets using research and development (R&D) expenditures and advertising expenditures in relation to book assets. The multinational discount may be partially explained if MNCs engage in excessive R&D and advertising expenditures which do not lead to creation of intangible assets. Our results, however, suggest that R&D expenditures raise Tobin's q equally for MNCs and DCs and that advertising expenditures raise q for MNCs but not for DCs. Furthermore, the multinational discount is unaffected even when controlling for R&D and advertising expenses, as well as other proxies for intangible assets and unobservable investment opportunities.

This paper proceeds with Section 2, which discusses the data and our different measures of multinationality, and takes a preliminary look at corporate multinationality. Section 3 presents the evidence that multinationality destroys relative firm value and estimates the magnitude of the multinational discount. It also presents the evidence on value creation through exporting and on multinational empire building by managers who do not own much of the firm. Section 4 considers the alternative hypotheses for the multinational discount.

2. A preliminary look at multinationality

Our analysis is based on a sample of U.S. nonfinancial firms from the Compustat database over the period 1984-1997, the longest period for which we could access Compustat data on multinationality. This yields 42,529 firm-year observations, of which 11,366 or 27% can be classified as MNCs on the basis of self-reported information on foreign operations.[4]

We focus on three main measures of multinationality which have typically been used in the international finance literature: (1) the ratio of sales from foreign operations to total sales, which we refer to as the "foreign sales ratio"; (2) a dummy variable for MNCs which equals one if the company reported any foreign sales and equals zero otherwise; and (3) the number of foreign countries in which the firm has operations, or the "country count". The amount of foreign sales is available annually from Compustat. The country count is taken from the *Directory of American Firms Operating in Foreign Countries* (1984, 1994), compiled only for 1984 and 1994, and is available for only a subset of companies in the Compustat database.[5] Table 1 demonstrates that these

---

[4] Note that our large panel includes both MNCs and DCs and thus allows us to identify differences between the two groups. Agmon and Lessard (1977), Errunza and Senbet (1984), and Reeb, Kwok, and Baek (1998) do not include DCs in their analysis.

[5] The *Directory* lists 119 and 121 countries in which U.S. firms have operations for 1984 and 1994, respectively. Although these data are not available annually, they could also be collected for 1987, 1991, and 1996. However, the data for 1984 and 1994 are highly correlated, at 0.86, so we do not expend labor collecting data for the intervening or subsequent years. For all years in 1984-1989 we use the country count for 1984, and for all years in 1990-1997 we use the country count from 1994.

three indicators of multinationality are positively correlated, but not strikingly so. Table 1 also shows the correlations between these multinationality measures and two supplementary measures of multinationality taken from Compustat (only for 1992-1997), the ratio of foreign assets to total assets ("foreign assets ratio") and the number of different geographic operating areas reported by the firm ("foreign segments").[6] These correlations are similar to those for the main measures, with the ratios of foreign sales and foreign assets being particularly correlated. The table also includes, for reference, the correlations between multinationality and the number of different industrial segments in which the firm operates (only for 1992-1997) and the ratio of exports to total sales (only for 1991-1997). These correlations reveal that while geographic and product diversification are correlated, they are certainly not the same, and that multinationality is completely unrelated to exporting. If exporting and multinational operations are substitutes, the difference in the location of assets (at home versus abroad) contains implications which we investigate later.

Multinationality has been rising during the time period under investigation. Figure 1 shows that the percent of sales from foreign operations has risen modestly for all firms from 6.5% in 1984 to around 8% in 1997. It also shows that the increase is more dramatic for the firms which are in the sample all 14 years, as their foreign sales have almost doubled from around 6.5% to 12% over the same time. The average number of foreign countries in which firms operate has also risen, albeit modestly, from 1.3 in 1984 to 1.4 in 1994 for all firms, and from 2.9 to 3.1 for firms in the sample each year.

Table 2 presents summary statistics for the three main measures of multinationality and also offers a comparison of MNCs with DCs across a number of additional characteristics. Panel A indicates that multinationals on average receive almost 29 percent of their revenue from foreign operations and operate in 11 different foreign countries. MNCs appear less leveraged than DCs (consistent with the findings of Fatemi (1988), Lee and Kwok (1988), and Burgman (1996)) and, not surprisingly, MNCs are clearly larger than DCs -- exhibiting statistically significantly greater market

---

[6] We also considered the ratio of foreign profits to total profits and the ratio of foreign taxes to total taxes, but rejected them as measures of multinationality because they are much more subject to accounting manipulation and because they commonly have negative numbers in the numerator which complicates interpretation.

equity, assets, and sales.[7] Panel B presents a break-down of the distribution of multinational firms across industry, and a χ^2 test strongly rejects the hypothesis that the distribution of MNCs and DCs is identical across industries. We therefore do not put much emphasis on the univariate comparisons of firm value, which are somewhat mixed depending on the measure used, and instead undertake an extensive investigation that controls for firm characteristics, including leverage, size, and industry.[8] The distribution of MNCs is much more stable over time, averaging around 27 percent and varying only from 26% to just under 29% in a given year. This stability in the percent of firms that have multinational operations somewhat hides the fact that the amount of foreign activity that these multinational firms have engaged in has been increasing, as discussed with reference to Figure 1.

3. The multinational discount, the asset channel of value destruction, and multinational empire building

3.1. The multinational discount on Tobin's q

Our main investigation of the relation between firm value and multinationality focuses on Tobin's q, which we take as our measure of relative firm value. This follows the approach adopted by Morck and Yeung (1991), Lang and Stulz (1994), Servaes (1996), Yermack (1996), and Allayannis and Weston (1999), among others.[9] We compute q as the sum of the market value of equity and the book value of debt divided by the book value of assets. We think about q as a weighted average of an unobserved q for domestic operations and an unobserved q for foreign operations, or the unobserved domestic q plus a weighted incremental contribution for

---

[7] Market equity, assets, and sales are all highly correlated. Using all firm-year observations, the correlation between the log of market equity and the log of assets is 0.88, the correlation between the log of market equity and the log of sales is 0.79, and the correlation between the log of assets and the log of sales is 0.91.

[8] The industries shown in panel B correspond to the set of dummy variables created to control for industry characteristics in the forthcoming analysis. We use annual industry dummy variables in the regressions.

[9] Lang and Stulz (1994) argue that Tobin's q is a useful measure of performance because it measures market value relative to replacement cost and is not a flow variable or return that needs to be risk-adjusted to compare across firms: "The advantage of Tobin's q is that it incorporates the capitalized value of the benefits from diversification."

multinationality: $q = (1 - w)q^d + wq^f = q^d + w(q^f - q^d)$.

Since section 2 pointed out that MNCs are less leveraged and larger than DCs, and that the industry composition is different for MNCs and DCs, we control for leverage using the lagged value of the ratio of debt to the sum of debt and market value of equity, control for size using the lagged value of the log of market equity (as in Fama and French (1992, 1993, 1995)), and control for industry using annual industry dummy variables. We use lagged values of size and leverage as independent variables so as to minimize potential endogeneity problems.[10]

The most important of the controls, as measured by adjusted R^2, is leverage, which is negatively related to q. The next most important control is the set of industry dummies. Size is only minimally important, although still with a significant (positive) impact on q.[11] The coefficients on the multinationality variables therefore measure the incremental contribution that multinationality makes to Tobin's q. The q of an otherwise similar domestic firm is thus the fitted value based only on size, leverage, and industry. This means that our estimated impact of multinationality can be viewed as the effect of the intensity of a firm's multinationality relative to the mean multinationality for that industry in that year, given other firm characteristics. Thus our results are not driven by cross-industry differences. Note that this approach differs from the "chop shop" approach often used to assess the domestic industrial diversification discount. The "chop shop" approach cannot be used to assess multinational operations because data on foreign operations does not provide sufficient detail to reliably identify the location of all foreign operations, and data on foreign corporations does not allow us to estimate comparable pure-play firms in each foreign country. Regardless, because the pure-play firms would be non-U.S. firms by definition, their valuation is unlikely to be relevant for U.S.-owned operations in those countries.

---

[10] We consider first-differenced regressions and additional control variables later.

[11] In a simple regression of q onto a constant and leverage, the adjusted R^2 is 0.20. (A quadratic specification including squared leverage as independent variables was also significant, suggesting that q is decreasing at an increasing rate in leverage ratio of 0.70, but the overall effect was not very different from the linear specification.) A regression of q onto 169 annual industry dummies produces an adjusted R^2 of 0.10, while a regression of q onto a constant and size yields an adjusted R^2 of only 0.02. Regressing q onto both leverage and the annual industry dummies results in an adjusted R^2 of 0.25, and including size slightly increases the adjusted R^2 to 0.26.

Table 3 presents the basic findings on the relation between relative firm value and multinationality. The regressions suggest that (the log of) Tobin's q is a decreasing function of multinationality for each of the three measures.[12] The coefficient on the MNC dummy implies that the multinational discount is 17.1 percent. The coefficients on the foreign sales ratio and on the country count indicate that the multinational discount is 8.6 and 11.7 percent, respectively.[13]

Taken together, the estimates for the average multinational discount are similar to estimates of the product-diversification discount found by Berger and Ofek (1995), which are in the 13 to 15 percent range (over 1985-1991). We therefore consider whether the multinational discount we find is simply the product diversification discount already known. The regressions at the far right of Table 3 re-estimate the basic regressions of Tobin's q but also control for the number of product segments in which the firm competes (for the period 1992-1997). Product diversification is found to lower Tobin's q, as expected. More importantly, inclusion of the product segment variable does not lower the estimates of the multinational discount and apparently even raises them (relative to the larger sample period). Hence, we conclude that the multinational discount is not simply the product diversification discount by proxy.

Although Table 3 replicates standard regressions in the MNC literature (see for example, Christophe (1997), Morck and Yeung (1991), Errunza and Senbet (1984, 1981)), we provide new evidence in two important ways. First, our large panel of recent data allows us to establish that multinationality destroys value in the late 1980s and 1990s, even if it did not in earlier time periods (as found, for instance, by Morck and Yeung (1991) using data for 1978). This supports the findings of Christophe (1997) who compares multinationality in the early 1980s with the late 1970s. Second, we use a variety of measures of multinationality where most prior work has examined the degree of

---

[12] Each of the estimated coefficients is significant at the 5 percent error level. The reported standard errors are heteroscedasticity-consistent, following White (1980). The results are similar when using heteroscedaticity and auto-correlation robust standard errors.

[13] A one percent increase in foreign sales is estimated to lower q by 0.299 percent. Since the average multinational in the sample has 28.7 percent foreign sales, the discount for the average firm is 8.6 percent. Similarly, each country of foreign operations lowers q by 1.1 percent. Since the average multinational operates in 10.65 countries, the discount for the average firm is 11.7 percent.

multinationality using only the proportion of foreign sales (to total sales). We confirm our findings using that variable with the MNC dummy and the country count.[14]

Additional results, not presented in tables, suggest that the multinational discount on Tobin's q is stable over the sample period. Splitting the sample into two sub-periods (1985-1989 and 1990-1997) provides coefficients on multinationality that are always statistically significantly negative and statistically identical across the two time periods. Similar results are also obtained using only the firms that are in the sample for all 14 years. Likewise, year-by-year cross-section regressions reveal that the multinational discount is present in each year of our sample, with the multinational coefficients consistently negative and significant.[15]

In addition to showing that multinationality reduces q, Table 3 also reports the impact of multinationality on the two components of q -- that is, assets (the denominator) and market value (the numerator). Not surprisingly, given the relation between firm size and multinationality, multinationals have larger assets and a greater market value (even after controlling for size, leverage, and industry-year effects). However, the component coefficient estimates reveal that MNCs have significantly more assets than they do market value compared to otherwise similar DCs and thus have less relative value. Using the MNC dummy, the ratio of the coefficients is 5.5 to 1. With the foreign sales ratio and the country count, the ratios of coefficients are 7.4 and 3.8 to 1, respectively. This result suggests that larger, less productive assets drive the multinational discount. We refer to this finding that multinationals have disproportionately high levels of assets as the *asset channel* of value destruction.

Because Tobin's q is only one of several measures of firm value, we also investigate the effect of multinationality on the ratio of book equity to market equity (and later investigate the

---

[14] Combining the multinationality variables in the regressions does not change the overall picture and the three are jointly significant However, the results do suggest that the simple MNC dummy is more important than the other variables.

[15] The coefficients vary in a narrow range from -0.208 to -0.122 for the MNC dummy, from -0.415 to -0.226 for the foreign sales ratio, and from -0.014 to -0.008 for the country count. Although these coefficients are fairly stable, simple regressions reveal that they are typically higher (in absolute value) in years when the dollar is strong. The role of exchange rates in the discount is discussed further in section 4.1.

price/earnings ratio, P/E, also). The results using the ratio of book equity to market equity are quite similar to results using q so are not reported separately. The multinational discount is in the range of 3.5 to 9.7 percent, somewhat lower than in the Tobin's q regressions. To generate this discount given the greater market value of MNCs, the impact of multinationality on book equity must be even larger. Hence, the asset channel of value destruction also appears as a book-equity channel.

The hypothesized asset channel of value destruction naturally raises the possibility that our measures of multinationality simply capture asset size -- e.g., perhaps tangible assets reduce Tobin's q rather than multinationality. Although we already control for overall firm size in the regressions, we divided the sample into high- and low-asset categories to examine the coefficients on multinationality. The multinational discount is present in all regressions (not reported). It turns out to be greater for firms in the low-asset half than in the high-asset half, suggesting that asset size does usurp part of the multinational discount. However, the premium for size (revealed in the coefficient on the lagged value of the log of market equity) is higher for firms in the low-asset half than in the high-asset half, suggesting that the higher multinational discount may be because q is proportionately high relative to size in the low-asset subsample anyway. Furthermore, we show later that foreign assets appear to destroy value and that changes in multinationality are significantly associated with similarly signed changes in assets -- and it is a more compelling story that increased multinationality causes increasing assets than vice versa.

3.2. Time series evidence

To establish more firmly the relation between q and multinationality we examine the relation between changes in those variables. This time-series evidence is strongly supportive of the cross-sectional evidence, and provides an important step towards a causal link between multinationality and value destruction. For example, it could be argued that MNCs are firms with less investment opportunities (which we explicitly assess later), or were poorly performing firms, and that this characteristic drives both their lower q's and their international operations. This is actually a difficult argument to make, because even after controlling for industry effects and firm-specific characteristics, we still find that multinationals are systematically low q.

Table 4, Panel A, uses the year-to-year changes to establish that increases in multinationality over the course of a year are strongly associated with decreases in relative value. In particular, a DC becoming an MNC on average suffers an almost 11% decline in relative value. A firm that increases its multinational sales by 10 percentage points suffers a 3% decline in relative value. (Because the country count is only observed for 1984 and 1994 it is omitted from this analysis.) The panel also confirms the role of the asset channel in the multinational discount. Increases in multinationality are concurrent with increases in assets that are much larger than the associated increases in market value (more than double for the MNC dummy and four times for the foreign sales ratio). More importantly, we supplement this finding by decomposing the assets of MNCs into their foreign and domestic components based on the firm's own allocations in standard SEC filings.[16] The regressions at the far right reveal that increases in the ratio of foreign assets to total assets particularly destroy firm value. In addition, they also reveal that increases in the number of foreign segements destroy value.

We also apply our time-series analysis over a much longer horizon to focus on the effect of more sustained changes in multinationality. Table 4, Panel B, examines changes in firms that were in the sample in both 1984 and 1997 (the first and last year respectively). For these firms, over that time period, increases in multinationality are indeed associated with significant decreases in firm value. The discount for becoming a multinational is about 14.5 percent, while a 10 percentage point increase in foreign sales reduces q by 4 percent and a new country of operation reduces q by 2 percent. Again we find further support for the asset channel, as increased multinationality is associated with much greater growth in assets than in market value.

The time series results reported here suggest that becoming a MNC or increasing the degree of existing multinational operations destroys firm value. The robustness of the asset channel to time-series analysis seems to support the interpretation that multinationality is driving down q, and not vice versa. This follows from the assumption that asset increases are a likely effect of increased foreign operations, but not the converse.

---

[16]We use the Compustat data on foreign assets. While accounting manipulations reduce the information content of this data, the problems are similar to that of allocating sales figures to foreign operations. Both are likely to be far superior to earnings data for foreign operations, which have additional tax motivation to be manipulated.

3.3. Earnings, asset productivity, and multinationality

To further investigate the hypothesized asset channel of value destruction, we now turn to earnings and the productivity of assets. Table 5 indicates that regressions of the P/E ratio imply a statistically significant multinational discount in the range from 2.3 to 4.3 percent. Since the multinational discount is larger with respect to Tobin's q and book-to-market-equity than for earnings, we can infer that the earnings of MNCs must be low relative to their levels of assets and book equity. We confirm this by examining the return on assets (ROA), which is indeed lower for multinationals based on the three measures of multinationality.[17] This suggests that ROA is lower for the foreign projects that MNCs undertake, or that assets and equity have to be relatively large for foreign projects in comparison to the earnings they generate. We provide an indirect test of this hypothesis by reconsidering the ratio of foreign assets to total assets. These results, also shown in Table 5, indicate that even when directly controlling for the amount of assets the firm has, the percentage of those assets that are foreign results in a lower ROA. This seems to confirm that it is particularly the foreign asset base, and therefore multinationality, that contributes to value destruction. Regressions with the other measures of multinationality, including the number of foreign segments reported by the firm support this.

We also find evidence, not reported here to conserve space, that earnings *growth* in not at all related to changes in multinationality, either on a year-to-year basis or on a 14-year basis (as considered in section 3.2). We conclude that firms increasing multinational operations increase their assets (as demonstrated in Table 4), but not their earnings, which may explain why market value does not increase as much as assets do.

3.4. Exporting and firm value

The hypothesis that extra, unproductive foreign assets are associated with multinationality can also be tested by investigating the effects of export activity, which can be viewed as a substitute for foreign operations that does not require foreign assets. In contrast to the discount associated with multinationality, we find that exporting is associated with value creation. Table 6 reports the results

---

[17] The results for the return on equity are similar but less significant.

using Tobin's q as the measure of firm value. Each percentage point of export sales raises q by 0.192%, such that the average exporting firm with 20.2% export sales has an *export premium* of 3.87%. The premium in q can be decomposed into the greater market value of the firm (by approximately 1.45 percent) for exporters, combined with a reduced asset size (by approximately 2.28 percent), which may reflect greater asset productivity. This is consistent with findings regarding the superior performance of exporting firms relative to non-exporting firms; e.g., Bernard and Jensen (1999) summarize this literature and present evidence that successful firms become exporters. Controlling for export activity in regressions of Tobin's q furthermore does not alter the multinational discount, as all the coefficients on the multinationality variables are statistically significantly negative and are of similar magnitude to the coefficients in regressions excluding the export ratio.

3.5. Multinational empire building by management

The evidence of a multinational discount leads us to consider why firms would become multinational or increase their degree of multinationality. Since the idea that multinationality destroys value is consistent with the growing body of research finding that other forms of diversification also destroy value, we borrow from that research for answers. Those studies – like this one – are suggestive that large expansions require large assets (or irreversible investments) that often do not generate a high enough return. An "empire building" motive has been ascribed to managers who pursue value-destroying diversification because of private benefits (see, for instance, Denis, Denis, and Sarin (1997), Stulz (1990), or Jensen (1986)). We investigate this potential explanation for the multinational discount by examining the role of management equity ownership in the determination of multinationality.[18] The results are presented in Table 7, which shows that management share ownership decreases the probability of being an MNC in logit and probit models. Furthermore, a one percentage point increase in management share ownership is associated with a

---

[18] The data on management share ownership is from the Execucomp database. Their data begins with year-end 1992 -- the date at which new disclosure requirements for executive compensation became effective -- and thus our sample period covers 1993-1997. Our data measure uses stock and stock options held by executive officers as a percentage of total shares outstanding (as in Fenn and Liang (1999)).

reduction in the percent of sales from foreign operations by three percentage points. Similar effects are found on the percent of foreign assets and on the number of foreign segments in which the firm operates. Although the other coefficients are not statistically significant, their signs suggest that an increase in management share ownership reduces the number of foreign countries in which the firm operates and reduces the likelihood the firm becomes a multinational. This evidence supports the hypothesis that managers of MNCs may be constructing multinational empires to the detriment of shareholders.

Our conclusion that value-destroying diversification is, in part, due to the private interest of managers is completely consistent with the findings of Denis, Denis, and Sarin (1997), who find a similar relationship between management share ownership and product diversification, Lang, Poulsen, and Stulz (1995), who conclude that management is reluctant to sell underperforming assets because they value firm size, and Morck, Shleifer, and Vishny (1990), who conclude that managers make diversifying acquisitions because they are maximizing personal objectives rather than shareholder value. Managers may benefit from diversification for a number of reasons associated with the trappings of managing a large far-flung empire, such as greater pay, power, responsibilities, and other forms of non-salary compensation such as prestige, decision-making freedom, travel, and human-capital accumulation.

4. Alternative hypotheses

4.1. Exchange rate effects

One potential source of the multinational discount in Tobin's q might be the value of the dollar during the period under investigation. To consider this, the regressions are augmented to include an interaction term between each measure of multinationality and the log of an exchange rate index. The results, presented in Table 8, indicate that a high value of the dollar (or low value of foreign currencies) destroys market value in relation to assets. The reported multinational coefficients are jointly significant, although not individually. The results are similar, but the statistical significance much stronger, when using the sub-sample of firms in existence for all 14

15

years, which provides for a longer time-series dimension of exchange rate fluctuations.[19]

Taking the sub-sample results, a 1% appreciation of the dollar lowers q for multinationals by almost 0.5 percent.[20] The total effect of multinationality on q is thus the coefficient on the measure of multinationality plus the product of the coefficient on the interaction term and the log of the exchange rate index. During this period, the dollar index averaged 107.299, so using the MNC dummy, the total effect of multinationality on q is an average discount of 12.6 percent. Even though dollar movements could destroy or augment value, the level effect implies that multinationality on average destroys value. In fact, in order to eliminate the multinational discount, the dollar would have to depreciate 25.7% to a level of 83.[21]

These results are important because, while completely consistent with conventional wisdom, previous literature has had difficulty in showing empirically a link between firm value and the exchange rate. Jorion (1990) and Ahimud (1994) find no relation between stock price movements and exchange rate changes. Christophe (1997) and Bartov, Bodnar, and Kaul (1996) can only make inferences between exchange rate fluctuations and valuation based on time period (Christophe) or equity volatility (Bartov, Bodnar, and Kaul). Unlike those papers, we find some statistically significant exchange rate effects.[22] We also provide evidence in Table 8 that changes in the dollar affect both market value and assets. There is a negative effect on market value, and a positive effect on assets. We speculate that the explanation for assets increasing with the value of the dollar might

_____

[19] Using this sub-sample is consistent with the suggestions of Bartov and Bodnar (1994) for reducing noise when examining exchange rate effects. By excluding new firms, the sub-sample reduces the weight on the most recent years, and might allow time for the market to learn about the firm's true exchange rate exposure.

[20] A dollar appreciation has a similar impact on firm value when interacted with exports.

[21] The estimated discount is 6.8 percent using the foreign sales ratio and 8.6 percent using the country count. Similar sized dollar depreciations would be required to reduce those estimated discounts to zero.

[22] Using changes in the variables (as in Table 5) we also find evidence of an exchange rate effect whereby dollar appreciations are associated with relative value reductions. As another test we examine whether the time-series of industry dummy variables from our basic regression (Table 4) are related to the exchange rate. For the full sample, there is no evidence of a relationship.

be that firms expand abroad when the dollar is strong and foreign assets are relatively cheaper to acquire.

In related research, firm earnings were not found to vary significantly with exchange rate interactions (and are thus not reported here). Hence, multinational firms may be smoothing their income -- via accounting manipulations, financial hedging, or operational hedging -- but financial markets adjust the firm's equity prices regardless.

4.2. Multinational risk

This section considers an alternative explanation for the multinational discount which we refer to as the *risk channel*. If MNCs are riskier than otherwise similar DCs because of exchange risk and political risk associated with their foreign projects, domestic shareholders may not want to hold MNC stocks when they can hold safer DC stocks instead -- an extreme version of home bias. As a result, MNC stocks might trade at a discount compared to DC stocks as an inducement to hold MNCs, and the expected rate of return on MNCs would be higher to compensate for the additional risks. This argument implies that the portfolio value to shareholders of the international diversification provided by MNCs is less than the costs of their greater risks, and additionally depends on the inability of shareholders to diversify or hedge these additional risks effectively or cheaply. In related research, Allayannis and Weston (1999) find that firms which hedge using foreign currency derivatives have higher Tobin's q than firms which do not hedge. This *hedging premium* – of about 6.7% – suggests that the absence of hedging causes a *risk discount*.

Table 9 reveals that MNC stocks are indeed more volatile than DC stocks, and primarily because of exchange rate volatility. Coefficients on the sales ratio and the country count are statistically significantly positive; the coefficient on the MNC dummy is negative but insignificant. To more fully consider the influence of exchange rate risk, we introduce an interaction term between each indicator of multinationality and the standard deviation of monthly percentage changes in the exchange rate index. Results indicate that the volatility of MNCs is higher when exchange rate volatility is higher. The MNC dummy suggests that the standard deviation of multinational returns is lower by 0.317 percentage points, but higher by 0.109 percentage points for every percentage point increase in the standard deviation of exchange rate changes -- on average yielding a reduction in risk.[23]   Otherwise, both the foreign sales ratio and the country count imply that increased multinational activity increases the equity volatility.

We conclude that multinationality tends to increase equity volatility, and that exchange rate volatility is the major contributor. While MNC equity returns are more volatile, our investigations of the volatility of earnings, earnings-per-share, and sales reveal that these income statement items are *not* more volatile for MNCs than for DCs. (In order to conserve space, these null results are not presented here.) One reason for this could be that firms seek to smooth their income or sales through accounting manipulations or by hedging, but, as suggested in the prior section, markets adjust the value of the firm regardless.

To consider a risk channel of value destruction as an explanation for the multinational discount, we directly tested whether either equity volatility or foreign exchange volatility are (negative) determinants of Tobin's q. Regressions reveal that neither factor is a negative determinant of Tobin's q, and that the negative coefficients on multinationality are not affected by their inclusion in the equation, and once again the null results are not presented here.[24]   Hence, we conclude that there is no evidence supporting the risk channel of value destruction or a risk discount, and that volatility cannot explain the multinational discount.

The findings that multinationality increases riskiness and destroys value raise the question of the impact of multinationality on stock returns. For example, regardless of the source of the multinational discount, multinationality may lower the relative market value of the firm enough to produce stock returns that are comparable to or higher than returns on purely domestic firms despite lower earnings. We thoroughly considered these impacts, but do not find convincing evidence of any differences in returns between MNCs and DCs, although there is some weak evidence that MNCs have higher returns.[25]   Furthermore, we do find evidence that equity returns are affected by

---

[23] The average standard deviation of the exchange rate index is 1.2 percentage points.

[24] We also interact foreign exchange volatility with multinationality as in Table 9, and again get insignificant results.

[25] The return regressions controlled for beta, firm size, book-to-market ratio, and leverage. Equations using the country count suggest that the returns for MNCs may be higher. Regressions using the country count also suggest that MNCs' Sharpe ratio may be higher, although the other

18

exchange rate changes, which is, of course, consistent with our finding on the effect of exchange rate changes on market value.

4.3. Intangible assets

Tobin's q, as a measure of relative market value, in part measures the value of the firm's intangible assets. Some authors have argued that the benefits of multinationality are derived from firm-specific capital such as a brand name or proprietary research (see Morck and Yeung (1991, 1999), Dunning (1981), and Hymer (1976)). Therefore, we include research and development (R&D) expenses (as a ratio to assets) and advertising expenses (as a ratio to assets) in our basic model to control for these intangibles. Table 10 shows that multinationality destroys value even when taking into account the R&D and advertising intensity of the firm. We find that both measures of intangibles have a positive effect on firm value, but only R&D is statistically significant. Considering whether the measures have a differential effect on MNCs and DCs, we find that R&D may destroy value in MNCs relative to DCs, while advertising adds significant value for MNCs relative to DCs.

As shown in Table 10, we also investigated additional controls for intangible assets, or unobserved investment opportunities. We add the P/E ratio to capture expected future growth, a dummy variable for whether dividends were paid out as a proxy for whether the firm is cash constrained, and the firm's investment intensity relative to its assets to capture investment opportunities. Including these additional controls, which all significantly suggest that firms with growth opportunities have greater value, does not change the value destruction result and typically strengthens its significance. Similar results hold using the two supplementary measures of multinationality.

5. Conclusions

Corporations have been forced to deal with an increasingly global environment over the past

---

measures of multinationality do not significantly impact returns or the Sharpe ratio. However, because these effects are weak and not systematic across our measures, we do not attach much importance to them.

few decades, and the general trend has been for firms to increase their multinationality. Evidence presented in this paper suggests that firms need to assess their international operations more carefully, as multinationality is on average associated with a discount on Tobin's q of 8.6% to 17.1% compared to domestic firms with similar characteristics. The multinational discount is also directly related to a firm's degree of multinationality and is similarly present other measures of relative value.

The main mechanism of value destruction appears to be an asset channel whereby multinationality requires extensive assets, particularly in relation to the earnings they generate. Multinationality is actually associated with a slight positive effect on firm value, but is also associated with a much larger positive effect on the asset base of the firm (in a ratio of about five to one). Although multinationality is also associated with slightly higher earnings, it is in fact associated with a reduction in the return on assets. Thus, the multinational discount is probably attributable to this relatively inefficient use of assets. By comparison, exporting from U.S. operations, an alternative to foreign operations which does not require foreign assets, is associated with a higher market value and a lower asset size. Additional evidence demonstrates that increases in multinationality are associated with decreases in firm value, suggesting that multinationality is causal in destroying value. Finally, we provide documentation that the greater the share of a firm owned by management, the less likely it is to be a multinational, implying that managers of multinationals are constructing multinational empires for private benefit at the expense of the shareholders.

References

Allayannis, George, and James P. Weston, "The Use of Foreign Currency Derivatives and Firm Market Value," manuscript, The University of Virginia, June 1999.

Amihud, Yakov, "Exchange Rates and the Valuation of Equity Shares," in *Exchange Rates and Corporate Performance*, edited by Yakov Amihud and Richard M. Levich, Irwin, 1994.

Agmon, Tamir, and Donald R. Lessard, "Investor Recognition of Corporate International Diversification," *Journal of Finance*, vol. 32, 1977, pp. 1049-1055.

Bartov, Eli, and Gordon M. Bodnar, "Firm Valuation, Earnings Expectations, and the Exchange-Rate Exposure Effect," *Journal of Finance*, vol. 49, 1994, pp. 1755-1785.

Bartov, Eli, Gordon M. Bodnar, and Aditya Kaul, "Exchange Rate Variability and the Riskiness of U.S. Multinational Firms: Evidence from the Breakdown of the Bretton Woods System," *Journal of Financial Economics*, vol. 42, 1996, pp. 105-132.

Berger, Philip G., and Eli Ofek, "Diversification's Effect on Firm Value," *Journal of Financial Economics*, vol. 37, 1995, pp. 39-65.

Bernard, Andrew B., and J. Bradford Jensen, "Exceptional Exporter Performance: Cause, Effect, or Both?" *Journal of International Economics*, vol. 47, 1999, pp. 1-25.

Bodnar, Gordon M., Charles Tang, and Joseph Weintrop, "Both Sides of Corporate Diversification: The Value Impacts of Geographic and Industrial Diversification," NBER Working Paper No. 6224, 1997.

Brewer, H.L., "Investor Benefits from Corporate International Diversification," *Journal of Financial and Quantitative Analysis*, vol. 16, 1981, pp. 113-126.

Burgman, Todd, "An Empirical Examination of Multinational Corporate Capital Structure," *Journal of International Business Studies*, vol. 27, 1996, pp. 553-570.

Christophe, Stephen E., "Hysteresis and the Value of the U.S. Multinational Corporation," *Journal of Business*, vol. 70, 1997, pp. 435-462.

Comment, Robert, and Gregg A. Jarrell, "Corporate Focus and Stock Returns," *Journal of Financial Economics*, vol. 37, 1995, pp. 67-87.

Denis, David J., Diane K. Denis, and Atulya Sarin, "Agency Problems, Equity Ownership, and Corporate Diversification," *Journal of Finance*, vol. 52, 1997, pp. 135-159.

Directory of American Firms Operating in Foreign Countries, 10th edition, Uniworld Business Publications, New York, 1984.

Directory of American Firms Operating in Foreign Countries, 13th edition, Uniworld Business Publications, New York, 1994.

Doukas, John, and Nickolas G. Travlos, "The Effect of Corporate Multinationalism on Shareholders' Wealth: Evidence from International Acquisitions," *Journal of Finance*, vol. 43, 1988, pp. 1161-1175.

Dunning, John, *International Production and the Multinational Enterprise*, George Allen and Unwin, 1981.

Errunza, Vihang R., and Lemma W. Senbet, "The Effects of International Operations on the Market Value of the Firm: Theory and Evidence," *Journal of Finance*, vol. 36, 1981, pp. 401-417.

Errunza, Vihang R., and Lemma W. Senbet, "International Corporate Diversification, Market Valuation, and Size-Adjusted Evidence," *Journal of Finance*, vol. 34, 1984, pp. 727-745.

Fama, Eugene F., and Kenneth R. French, "The Cross-Section of Expected Stock Returns," *Journal of Finance*, vol. 47, 1992, pp. 427-465.

Fama, Eugene F., and Kenneth R. French, "Common Risk Factors in the Returns on Stocks and

Bonds," *Journal of Financial Economics*, vol. 33, 1993, pp. 3-56.

Fama, Eugene F., and Kenneth R. French, "Size and Book-to-Market Factors in Earnings and Returns," *Journal of Finance*, vol. 50, 1995, pp. 131-155.

Fatemi, Ali M., "Shareholder Benefits from Corporate International Diversification," *Journal of Finance*, vol. 34, 1984, pp. 1325-1344.

Fatemi, Ali M., "The Effect of International Diversification on Corporate Financing Policy," *Journal of Business Research*, vol. 16, 1988, pp. 17-30.

Fenn, George W., and Nellie Liang, "Corporate Payout Policy and Managerial Stock Incentives," manuscript, 1999.

Gleason, Kimberly C., Ike Mathur, and Manohar Singh, "International Focus Enhancing Strategies: The Evidence from Divestments of Foreign Assets by U.S. Firms," manuscript, 1999.

Hughes, John S., Dennis E. Logue, and Richard James Sweeney, "Corporate International Diversification and Market Assigned Measures of Risk and Diversification," *Journal of Financial and Quantitative Analysis*, vol. 10, 1975, pp. 627-637.

Hymer, Stephen H., *The International Operations of National Firms: A Study of Direct Foreign Investment*, MIT Press, 1976.

Jensen, Michael C., "Agency Costs of Free Cash Flow, Corporate Finance, and the Market for Takeovers," *American Economic Review*, vol. 76, 1986, pp. 323-329.

John, Kose, and Eli Ofek, "Asset Sales and Increases in Focus," *Journal of Financial Economics*, vol. 37, 1995, pp. 105-126.

Jorion, Philippe, "The Exchange-Rate Exposure of U.S. Multinationals," *Journal of Business*, vol. 63, 1990, pp. 331-345.

Lang, Larry, Annette Poulsen, and Rene Stulz, "Asset Sales, Firm Performance, and the Agency Costs of Managerial Discretion," *Journal of Financial Economics*, vol. 37, 1995, pp. 3-37.

Lang, Larry H. P., and Rene M. Stulz, "Tobin's *q*, Corporate Diversification, and Firm Performance," *Journal of Political Economy*, vol. 102, 1994, pp. 1248-1280.

Lee, Kwang Chul, and Chuck C.Y. Kwok, "Multinational Corporations vs. Domestic Corporations: International Environmental Factors and Determinants of Capital Structure," *Journal of International Business Studies*, vol. 19, 1988, pp. 195-217.

Morck, Randall, Andrei Shleifer, and Robert W. Vishny, "Do Managerial Objectives Drive Bad Acquisitions?" *Journal of Finance*, vol. 45, 1990, pp. 31-48.

Morck, Randall, and Bernard Yeung, "Why Investors Value Multinationality," *Journal of Business*, vol. 64, 1991, pp. 165-187.

Morck, Randall, and Bernard Yeung, "Why Firms Diversify: Internalization vs. Agency Behavior," manuscript, 1999.

Reeb, David M., Chuck C.Y. Kwok, H. Young Baek, "Systematic Risk of the Multinational Corporation," *Journal of International Business Studies*, vol. 29, 1998, pp. 263-279.

Servaes, Henri, "The Value of Diversification During the Conglomerate Merger Wave," *Journal of Finance*, vol. 51, 1996, pp. 1201-1225.

Stulz, Rene M., "Managerial Discretion and Optimal Financing Policies," *Journal of Financial*

Economics, vol. 26, 1990, pp. 3-28.

White, Halbert, "A Heteroskedasticity-Consistent Covariance Matrix Estimator and Direct Test for Heteroskedasticity," *Econometrica*, vol. 48, 1980, pp. 817-838.

Yermack, David, "Higher Market Valuation of Companies with a Small Board of Directors," *Journal of Financial Economics*, vol. 40, 1996, 185-211.

FIGURE 1

PERCENT OF SALES FROM FOREIGN OPERATIONS

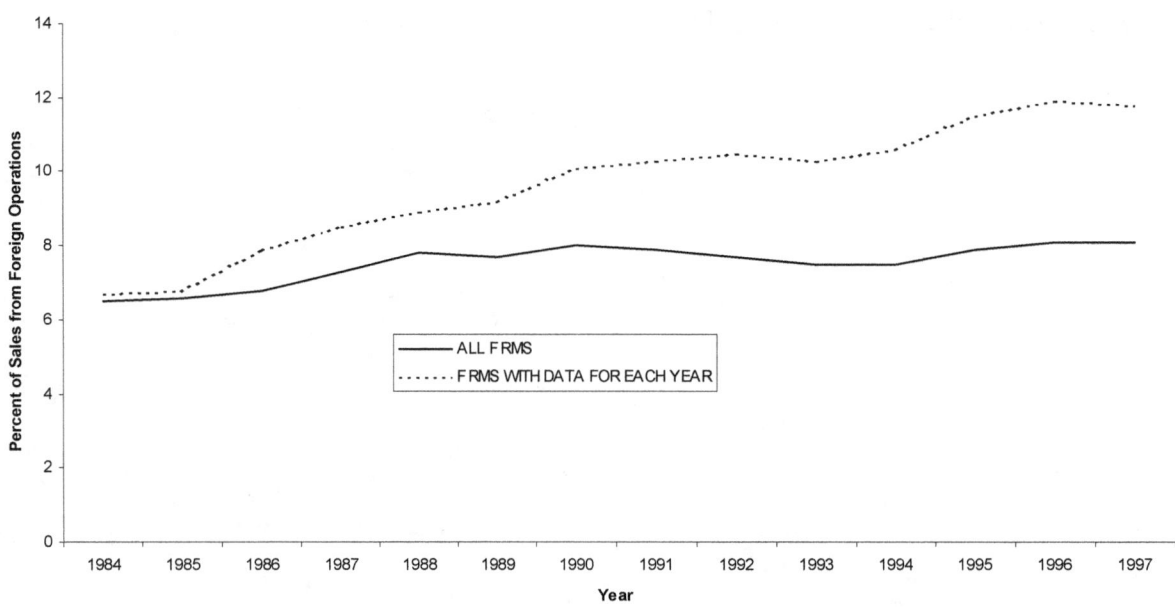

TABLE 1

CORRELATIONS BETWEEN DIFFERENT MEASURES OF MULTINATIONALITY
(Using firm-year observations)

The table shows the correlations between the three main measures of multinationality, two supplementary measures of multinationality (which are observed for a smaller time period), and two measures of potentially related corporate activity. The foreign sales ratio is sales from foreign operations divided by total sales. The MNC dummy variable is an indicator derived from the foreign sales ratio. The country count is the number of foreign countries in which the firm has operations. The foreign assets ratio is assets assigned to foreign operations divided by total assets. Foreign segments is the number of different geographic operating areas reported by the firm. Product segments is the number of different industrial operating areas reported by the firm. The export ratio is U.S. export sales divided by total sales. All correlations are significant at the 1 percent error level, except for the export ratio with the country count and with the foreign assets ratio, both of which are significant at the 10 percent error level. The number of observations used in each calculation appears in parentheses below the correlation.

	main measures of multinationality			supplementary measures of multinationality		potentially related activities	
	foreign sales ratio (1984-1997)	MNC dummy (1984-1997)	country count (1984-1997)	foreign assets ratio (1992-1997)	foreign segments (1992-1997)	product segments (1992-1997)	export ratio (1991-1997)
MNC dummy	0.75 (42529 obs)						
country count	0.67 (35876 obs)	0.62 (35876 obs)					
foreign assets ratio	0.91 (25259 obs)	0.75 (25830 obs)	0.66 (21941 obs)				
foreign segments	0.73 (24408 obs)	0.88 (27236 obs)	0.67 (22219 obs)	0.77 (25830 obs)			
product segments	0.09 (23925 obs)	0.18 (24408 obs)	0.29 (19908 obs)	0.13 (23702 obs)	0.19 (24408 obs)		
export ratio	-0.02 (28818 obs)	0.03 (28818 obs)	-0.01 (23997 obs)	-0.01 (25823 obs)	0.02 (27229 obs)	-0.05 (24401 obs)	

27

TABLE 2
CHARACTERISTICS OF MULTINATIONALITY
(Using firm-year observations, 1984-1997)

A. MULTINATIONALS COMPARED TO DOMESTIC CORPORATIONS
(* and ** denote significance at 10% and 5% error levels, respectively.)

VARIABLE	Mean for MNCs	Mean for DCs	t-Test of Equality
foreign sales ratio (# of obs.)	0.287 (11366)	0.000 (31163)	230.597**
MNC dummy (# of obs.)	1.0 (11366)	0.0 (31163)	NA
country count (# of obs.)	10.65 (4173)	0.00 (31163)	150.354**
Tobin's q (log)	0.224	0.294	-8.324**
book/market (log)	-0.754	-0.743	-1.107
P/E ratio (log)	2.946	2.921	2.410**
leverage	23.1 %	24.2 %	-4.104**
market equity (log)	5.607	3.993	69.712**
assets (log)	5.701	4.065	72.390**
sales (log)	5.749	3.924	72.748**

B. DISTRIBUTION OF MULTINATIONAL FIRMS BY INDUSTRY

SIC CODES	INDUSTRY DESCRIPTION	# of MNCs	TOTAL # of firms	% MNC
0000-0999	Agriculture	32	165	19 %
1000-1999	Mining and Construction	658	2623	25 %
2000-2199	Food and Tobacco	288	1209	24 %
2200-2399	Textiles and Apparel	188	910	21 %
2400-2799	Lumber, Furniture, and Paper	629	1992	32 %
2800-2999	Chemicals	1403	3600	39 %
3000-3299	Rubber, Leather, Stone, and Glass	485	1268	38 %
3300-3499	Metals	554	1694	33 %
3500-3699	Machinery, Computers, Electronics	2828	7146	40 %
3700-3999	Transportation Equipment	1827	5051	36 %
4000-4999	Transportation and Communications	446	4523	10 %
5000-5999	Wholesale and Retail Trade	657	5533	12 %
7000-8999	Services	1371	6815	20 %
	TOTAL	11366	42529	27 %

28

TABLE 3

MULTINATIONALITY AS A DETERMINANT OF FIRM VALUE, 1985-1997

(Heteroscedasticity-Consistent Standard Errors in Parentheses; * and ** denote significance at 10% and 5% error levels, respectively.)

Tobin's q is calculated as the market value of the firm (market value of equity plus book value of debt) divided by book value of assets, and enters the regressions in logarithmic form. The measures of multinationality are as described in Table 1. Regressions control for firm size (using the lagged value of log of market equity and debt), leverage (using the lagged value of the ratio of debt to the sum of market equity and debt), and industry (using annual industry dummy variables for the 13 categories listed in Table 3, not reported here). Regressions of the log of assets and the log of market value show the impact on the denominator and numerator of Tobin's q, respectively. The last set of regressions controls for the firm's product diversification via the number of different reported product segments in which the firm produces (this data is only from 1992-1997).

dependent variable	TOBIN'S q — ln q	TOBIN'S q — ln q	COMPONENTS OF q — ln assets	COMPONENTS OF q — ln market value	COMPONENTS OF q — ln market value	CONTROL FOR PRODUCT DIVERSIFICATION, 1992-1997 — ln q	CONTROL ... — ln q	CONTROL ... — ln q
MNC dummy	−0.171** (.008)		0.208** (.008)	0.038** (.007)		−0.383** (.015)		
foreign sales ratio	−0.299** (.022)		0.346** (.023)	0.047** (.019)			−0.466** (.030)	
country count		−0.011** (.001)	0.015** (.001)		0.004** (.000)			−0.034** (.002)
product segments						−0.236** (.007)	−0.242** (.006)	−0.223** (.008)
lagged firm size	0.049** (.002)	0.045** (.002)	0.927** (.002) / 0.936** (.002)	0.975** (.002) / 0.978** (.002)	0.972** (.002)	0.192** (.003)	0.181** (.003)	0.196** (.004)
lagged firm leverage	−1.178** (.017)	−1.176** (.018)	2.957** (.017) / 2.978** (.017)	1.777** (.017) / 1.782** (.017)	1.798** (.018)	−1.812** (.060)	−1.817** (.059)	−1.699** (.062)
number of observations	35228	29672	35228	35228	29672	23829	23829	19820
adjusted R²	0.27	0.27	0.92	0.94	0.94	0.27	0.27	0.27

29

TABLE 4. CHANGE IN MULTINATIONALITY AS A DETERMINANT OF CHANGE IN TOBIN'S q
(Heteroscedasticity-Consistent Standard Errors in Parentheses; * and ** denote significance at 10% and 5% error levels, respectively.)

The dependent variable and measures of multinationality enter as changes over 1 or 13 years. Annual regressions include annual industry dummy variables, and 13-year regressions include industry dummy variables. Annual regressions control for firm size and leverage using the lagged change in the log of market equity and the lagged change in leverage, and 13-year regressions control for firm size and leverage using the initial value of the log of market equity and leverage. The annual regressions are supplemented with two measures of the change in the firm's foreign assets. The foreign asset ratio is the percentage of assets in foreign operations to total assets and the foreign segments is the number of reported foreign operating segments (this data is only for 1992-1997).

A. ANNUAL CHANGES, 1985-1997

dependent variable	q growth		asset growth		market value growth		q growth (1992-1997)	
Δ MNC dummy	-10.91** (2.43)		21.09** (1.397)		10.18** (2.60)			
Δ foreign sales ratio		−0.003** (.0005)		0.004** (.0003)		0.001** (.0006)		
Δ foreign asset ratio							-23.46** (8.58)	
Δ foreign segments								-8.968** (1.97)
lag Δ ln size	-0.169** (.005)	-0.169** (.005)	0.137** (.003)	0.137** (.003)	-0.029** (.006)	-0.029** (.006)	-0.161** (.007)	-0.160** (.006)
lag Δ leverage	0.005** (.0006)	0.005** (.0006)	0.003** (.0003)	0.003** (.0003)	0.007** (.0007)	0.007** (.0007)	0.003** (.001)	0.003** (.001)
number of obs.	30996	30996	30996	30996	30996	30996	16523	16523
adjusted R^2	0.09	0.09	0.08	0.08	0.06	0.06	0.06	0.06

B. 13-YEAR CHANGES FROM 1984 TO 1997, FOR FIRMS IN SAMPLE ALL 14 YEARS

dependent variable	q growth			asset growth			market value growth		
Δ MNC dummy	-14.50** (6.05)			42.97** (7.07)			28.47** (9.06)		
Δ sales ratio		-0.004** (.002)			0.009** (.002)			0.005* (.003)	
Δ country count			-2.062** (.870)			0.657 (1.02)			-1.406 (1.32)
ln size, 1984	0.001* (.0008)	0.002* (.0008)	0.001 (.0015)	-0.001 (.0009)	-0.002* (.008)	-0.001 (.002)	-0.000 (.019)	-0.000 (.019)	-0.001 (.002)
leverage, 1984	23.09** (2.00)	22.98** (2.00)	22.45** (2.48)	-10.36** (2.34)	-9.98** (2.35)	-7.18** (2.91)	12.73** (3.00)	13.00** (3.01)	15.27** (3.74)
number of obs.	996	996	640	984	996	640	996	996	640
adjusted R^2	0.16	0.16	0.16	0.06	0.05	0.02	0.04	0.04	0.05

30

TABLE 5

MULTINATIONALITY AND EARNINGS, 1985-1997

(Heteroscedasticity-Consistent Standard Errors in Parentheses; * and ** denote significance at 10% and 5% error levels, respectively.)

The return on assets (ROA) is calculated as the year's income before extraordinary items divided by the beginning-of-year book value of assets. The foreign asset ratio is the percentage of assets in foreign operations to total assets and the foreign segments is the number of reported operating segments (this data is only for 1992-1997). Regressions control for firm size, leverage, and industry.

dependent variable	EARNINGS DISCOUNT			CASH FLOW AND MULTINATIONALITY			CASH FLOW AND FOREIGN ASSETS (1992-1997)	
	ln P/E	ln P/E	ln P/E	ROA	ROA	ROA	ROA	ROA
MNC dummy	-0.037** (.013)			-0.037 (.032)				
foreign sales ratio		-0.073* (.038)			-0.102* (.052)			
country count			-0.004** (.001)			-0.009** (.003)		
foreign asset ratio							-0.037* (.021)	
foreign segments								-0.013** (.003)
lagged ln mk val	0.017** (.003)	0.015** (.003)	0.018** (.003)					
lagged ln assets				0.075** (.007)	0.079** (.005)	0.087** (.008)	0.064** (.002)	0.065** (.002)
lagged leverage	-0.842** (.031)	-0.845** (.031)	-0.850** (.034)	-0.0001 (.0003)	-0.0001 (.0003)	-0.0001 (.0004)	-0.078** (.025)	-0.079** (.025)
number of obs.	24722	24722	20730	34759	34759	29234	19594	19594
adjusted R²	0.10	0.10	0.10	0.01	0.01	0.01	0.13	0.13

TABLE 6

EXPORTING AS A DETERMINANT OF TOBIN'S q, 1991-1997

(Heteroscedasticity-Consistent Standard Errors in Parentheses; * and ** denote significance at 10% and 5% error levels, respectively.)

The export sales ratio is U.S. export sales divided by total sales. Regressions control for firm size, leverage, and industry/year effects (significant, but not reported).

dependent variable	ln q				ln assets				ln market value			
export sales ratio	0.192** (.041)	0.166** (.063)	0.157** (.041)	0.172** (.046)	-0.113** (.040)	-0.081** (.040)	-0.073* (.040)	-0.107** (.045)	0.072** (.036)	0.078** (.036)	0.077** (.036)	0.058 (.040)
MNC dummy		-0.175** (.010)				0.214** (.010)				0.039** (.009)		
foreign sales ratio			-0.292** (.027)				0.330** (.027)				0.038* (.023)	
country count				-0.012** (.001)				0.017** (.001)				0.005** (.001)
lagged value of ln market equity	0.041** (.002)	0.055** (.002)	0.048** (.002)	0.051** (.003)	0.929** (.003)	0.912** (.003)	0.921** (.003)	0.912** (.003)	0.970** (.002)	0.967** (.003)	0.969** (.003)	0.962** (.003)
lagged value of leverage	-1.220** (.020)	-1.186** (.020)	-1.205** (.020)	-1.177** (.022)	3.040** (.021)	3.000** (.021)	3.024** (.021)	3.010** (.023)	1.817** (.021)	1.810** (.021)	1.815** (.021)	1.829** (.023)
number of observations	24514	24504	24504	20410	24557	24547	24547	20443	24519	24509	24509	20415
adjusted R²	0.26	0.26	0.26	0.26	0.91	0.91	0.91	0.91	0.93	0.93	0.93	0.93

TABLE 7
MANAGEMENT SHARE OWNERSHIP AS A DETERMINANT OF MULTINATIONALITY, 1993-1997

(Heteroscedasticity-Consistent Standard Errors in Parentheses; * and ** denote significance at 10% and 5% error levels, respectively.)

The dependent variables are the different measures of multinationality. The independent variable of interest is the quantity of shares owned by firm management in relation to total shares outstanding, from the Execucomp Database. The regressions also control for firm size, leverage, the ratio of book equity to market equity, and annual industry effects (not reported). Significance for the limited dependent regressions is determined using p-values from a Wald chi-square test.

Dependent Variable:	MNC Dummy	MNC Dummy	Foreign Sales Ratio	Country Count	Foreign Segments	Foreign Asset Ratio	Δ MNC Dummy
Model:	LOGIT	PROBIT	OLS	OLS	OLS	OLS	OLS
share of firm owned by top management	-0.577** (.176)	-0.352** (.103)	-3.097** (1.245)	-0.149 (.565)	-0.169** (.066)	-0.029** (.011)	-0.014 (.009)
log size	0.556** (.023)	0.320** (.013)	3.650** (.145)	2.539** (.064)	0.234** (.008)	0.034** (.001)	0.002** (.001)
leverage	-0.149** (.049)	-0.092** (.028)	-0.027 (.025)	0.041 (.044)	-0.002* (.001)	-0.001 (.001)	-0.0001 (.0002)
book/market	0.012** (.007)	0.008** (.004)	0.034 (.041)	-0.107 (.103)	0.004 (.002)	0.001 (.001)	0.0002 (.0003)
number of observations	6197	6197	6196	4827	6185	5768	6196
Chi-square for model fit, or adjusted R^2	1785**	1202**	0.24	0.37	0.31	0.23	0.01

TABLE 8

MULTINATIONALITY AND EXCHANGE RATES AS DETERMINANTS OF TOBIN'S q, 1985-1997

(Heteroscedasticity-Consistent Standard Errors in Parentheses; * and ** denote significance at 10% and 5% error levels, respectively.)

The dependent variables enter in logarithmic form. The exchange rate is the dollar index from the Federal Reserve Bank of Atlanta. The log of the exchange rate index is interacted with the measures of multinationality in order to assess the response of q to exchange rate changes in proportion to their level of multinationality. Regressions control for firm size, leverage, and industry as described in Tables 4 and 5.

dependent variable	ALL DATA			FIRMS IN SAMPLE ALL 14 YEARS								
	ln q	ln q	ln q	ln q	ln q	ln q	ln assets	ln assets	ln assets	ln market value	ln market value	ln market value
MNC dummy	0.009 (.494)			2.174** (.626)			-1.490** (.606)			0.682 (.451)		
MNC dummy × ln exchange rate	-0.039 (.106)			-0.492** (.135)			0.348** (.130)			-0.143 (.097)		
sales ratio		0.185 (1.603)			4.338** (2.075)			-1.175 (1.918)			3.164** (1.398)	
sales ratio × ln exchange rate		-0.104 (.345)			-0.982** (.447)			0.308 (.413)			-0.674** (.301)	
country count			0.024 (.036)			0.100** (.039)			-0.059 (.037)			0.041** (.020)
country count × ln exchange rate			-0.007 (.008)			-0.023** (.008)			0.014* (.008)			-0.008* (.004)
lagged value of ln market equity	0.049** (.002)	0.042** (.002)	0.045** (.002)	0.051** (.002)	0.047** (.002)	0.055** (.003)	0.937** (.002)	0.941** (.002)	0.931** (.003)	0.988** (.002)	0.989** (.002)	0.987** (.002)
lagged value of leverage	-1.178** (.017)	-1.195** (.017)	-1.176** (.018)	-1.083** (.024)	-1.096** (.024)	-1.099** (.027)	2.775** (.025)	2.789** (.025)	2.794** (.027)	1.692** (.022)	1.694** (.022)	1.695** (.024)
number of observations	35228	35228	29672	12876	12876	11191	12883	12883	11195	12876	12876	11191
adjusted R²	0.27	0.27	0.27	0.31	0.30	0.30	0.95	0.95	0.95	0.97	0.97	0.97

34

TABLE 9
MULTINATIONALITY AND EXCHANGE RATE VOLATILITY AS DETERMINANTS
OF THE STANDARD DEVIATION OF MONTHLY RETURNS, 1985-1995
(Heteroscedasticity-Consistent Standard Errors in Parentheses; * and ** denote significance at 10% and 5% error levels, respectively.)

The dependent variable is the annual standard deviation of the monthly stock return. Exchange rate volatility is the annual standard deviation of the monthly percentage change in the dollar index of the Federal Reserve Bank of Atlanta. Exchange rate volatility is interacted with the measures of multinationality in order to assess the response of a firm's stock risk to exchange rate risk in proportion to its level of multinationality. Regressions control for firm size, leverage, the ratio of book-equity to market-equity, and annual industry effects.

dependent variable	standard deviation of monthly equity returns					
MNC dummy	−0.079 (.087)			−0.317** (.104)		
MNC dummy × exch. rate volatility				0.109** (.029)		
sales ratio		0.841** (.243)			0.088 (.243)	
sales ratio × exch. rate volatility					0.325** (.088)	
country count			0.030** (.005)			0.018** (.006)
country count × exch. rate volatility						0.005** (.002)
lagged ln size	−1.716** (.024)	−1.744** (.023)	−1.790** (.027)	−1.717** (.024)	−1.744** (.023)	−1.791** (.027)
lagged ln book/market	−1.813** (.070)	−1.830** (.070)	−1.855** (.076)	−1.814** (.070)	−1.829** (.070)	−1.855** (.076)
lagged leverage	2.066** (.231)	2.033** (.231)	1.983** (.255)	2.075** (.231)	2.036** (.231)	1.985** (.255)
number of observations	24161	24161	20630	24161	24161	20630
adjusted R^2	0.35	0.35	0.36	0.35	0.35	0.36

TABLE 10
TOBIN'S q, MULTINATIONALITY, AND INTANGIBLE ASSETS, 1985-1997
(Heteroscedasticity-Consistent Standard Errors in Parentheses; * and ** denote significance at 10% and 5% error levels, respectively.)

The log of Tobin's q is regressed onto the measures of multinationality and the ratio of R&D expenditures to assets, the ratio of advertising expenditures to assets, the ratio of investment spending to assets, the P/E ratio, and a dummy variable for whether the firm paid dividends that year. Regressions also control for firm size, leverage, and annual industry effects.

dependent variable	Tobin's q					
MNC dummy	−0.204** (.010)			−0.232** (.011)		
foreign sales ratio		−0.404** (.027)			−0.369** (.025)	
country count			−0.011** (.001)			−0.019** (.001)
R & D	1.586** (.057)	1.604** (.058)	1.651** (.063)			
advertising	0.106 (.079)	0.092 (.078)	0.051 (.092)			
dividends paid				-0.258** (.011)	-0.265** (.011)	-0.247** (.012)
P/E ratio				0.271** (.006)	0.273** (.006)	0.273** (.006)
investment				0.705** (.055)	0.743** (.056)	0.676** (.059)
lagged ln size	0.063** (.002)	0.055** (.002)	0.057** (.003)	0.157** (.003)	0.148** (.003)	0.163** (.003)
lagged leverage	−1.105** (.022)	−1.128** (.022)	−1.108** (.024)	−0.079** (.006)	−0.080** (.006)	−0.077** (.006)
number of observations	23063	23063	18909	27115	27115	22166
adjusted R^2	0.32	0.32	0.32	0.32	0.32	0.33